THE PRAYING ATHLETE™
QUOTE BOOK

VOL 8
LIVING LIFE
PART 2

Unless otherwise indicated, Scripture quotations in this book are taken from The Holy Bible, *New International Version®, NIV®*. Copyright © 1973, 1978, 1984, 2011 by Biblica, Inc.™ Used by permission. All rights reserved worldwide.

Published by The Core Media Group, Inc., P.O. Box 2037, Indian Trail, NC 28079.

Cover & Interior Design: Ashlyn Helms

Printed in the United States of America.

VOL 8 LIVING LIFE
PART 2

Relationships are so much like
the ocean: back and forth, the
waves cleaning as they go.
Always be willing to
give and take with each
other along the way.

**Fans cool us off in the heat.
Sometimes we just need to be
quiet and stop producing
so much hot air.**

**What are you transporting in
your life that can be
dropped off to help someone
in his or her own life?**

A simple way to meet people: smile.

**Better solutions? Simple.
You speak, I listen,
I speak, you listen.**

If you have to choose between
right and wrong you must first
define the right and wrong
in your life and have a guide.
Allow the Bible to
be your guide.

Have you ever noticed how corn is planted so closely together? Unless it is planted closely together, the corn cannot grow. Each stalk helps the next stalk grow as they protect each other from storms.
Stay close to others and protect each other from the storms of life.

How do you know if you love someone? Pray for them, think about them, honor and respect them, trust them, and believe in them.

Finding freedom from past relationships is no easy task. The freedom you are looking for may not be possible because you cannot let go.

Building momentum in a relationship requires energy by both parties.

What are you pressing toward? It could be greatness or sadness. Two different roads, but both you can press. Choose your road today.

Our life is made up of seasons: good, bad, and some sad, but we all can protect the time we have to get better for those tough times.

As a leader, you can steer the conversation. If you want to be better, steer it better.

**Put on your emotional armor
as you serve your team.**

Listen to your discerning heart.

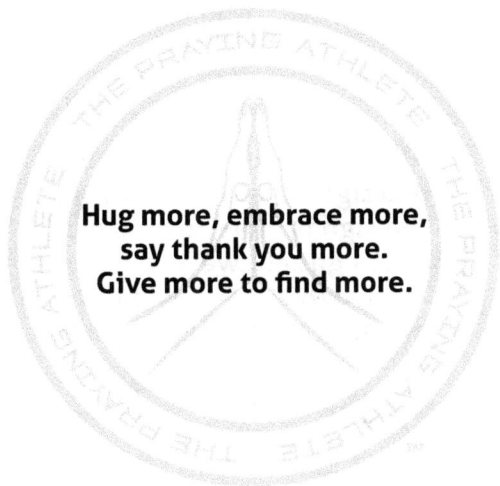

**Hug more, embrace more,
say thank you more.
Give more to find more.**

Have you ever missed the road sign? Missed your turn? The sign is there to help us. What signs are we missing in our own lives to enable us to get back on the right path?

Find a way to give back to
those who have given to you.
It can be big or small—
maybe just a card to say,
"I appreciate you more than
words could ever say or
explain, and you mean the
world to me." That is a great
start. It gets tiresome when
just one side is doing all the
giving. Everyone can give
something. You can give
your words, presence or time.
And that could be worth
more than any monetary gift
to some, because there
is no value for that.

Lighthouses help people and boats find their way. Be a lighthouse for someone today.

**Instead of crying about what
you do not have, take time
to go give something to
someone who does not have.**

When you have a passion to chase after God, you will find yourself doing and acting with more zeal and focus than others, and that is okay. They will either catch up with you one day or new people will come into your life to continue to push you on this journey.

Sometimes we need to accelerate to get to our next goal. Sometimes we need to park and get some rest. There are times we need to look back at God's blessing and goodness. And, there are times we need to let go and make sure God is guiding us. So, we put our lives in neutral and do not press on. However, to do any of the above for an extended time will cause us to lose our way. Find the balance you need in your life, and embrace each phase as a way to endure the race of life.

At one time, the
fax machine was an
incredible breakthrough in
technology. Now, it is almost
totally obsolete. Always
change and update
your skills to meet the
needs of tomorrow.

How can you decide what you want to be if you have not decided what you can be with God's help. You cannot do it alone.

Friends can be a hindrance or a blessing. Some friends never want you to succeed, so they will try to discourage you in their own manipulative way. Find the friends who will give you good counsel with no benefit for themselves, and you will find a friend for life.

Umbrellas have so many
purposes. It protects us
from rain, wind, hail, snow,
ice, and even the sun. But it
symbolizes much more than
that. It is a shelter in the
tough times and a place of
refuge. Keep your spiritual
umbrella, the word
of God, close by.
The storms of life are coming.

To be great you must believe in yourself. You must have a drive, be focused, be confident and grab all your energy to overcome the negative noise of the day. But the real, true key is to be so competitive that you rise up early to beat the birds to make the first beautiful sound of the day.

When you promise yourself
something and you focus
your efforts on attaining
your promise, one thing to
remember is the process to
achieve the promise will be
always be a challenge. The
promise you made cannot be
achieved without pushing
through your personal
process. Everyone's process
is different but one thing we
know is that it will not be
easy to achieve your promise
without a journey full of
processes. Buckle up!

If you have it within your sphere of influence to do good through encouragement, a helping hand, serving or giving, what should you do? Worry about how you may be perceived? Be concerned what someone may say? No! Do it! Changing a person's life is more important than anything you can accomplish. One small deed could give someone the will to push for another day, so DO IT.

Have faith my friend, He will deliver in His time. Allow Him to do His work, be careful not to circumvent His work with your work and your plans. Be patient. His work and timing will be much more beautiful than anything you can imagine or dream of, but you must first subject your will to His will. The first step is to engage faith. Make it real and purposeful in your life. When He does release you oh... hold on. Your heart will be overwhelmed with such joy, peace and total fulfillment, because the journey He has you on is the journey He wants to fulfill in your life. So what's your next move? Just have faith.

THOUGHTS & REFLECTIONS

_____

_____

_____

_____

_____

_____

_____

_____

_____

_____

_____

_____

_____

_____

_____

_____

_____

_____

_____

_____

_____

_____

_____

_____

_____

_____

_____

_____

_____

_____

_____

_____

_____

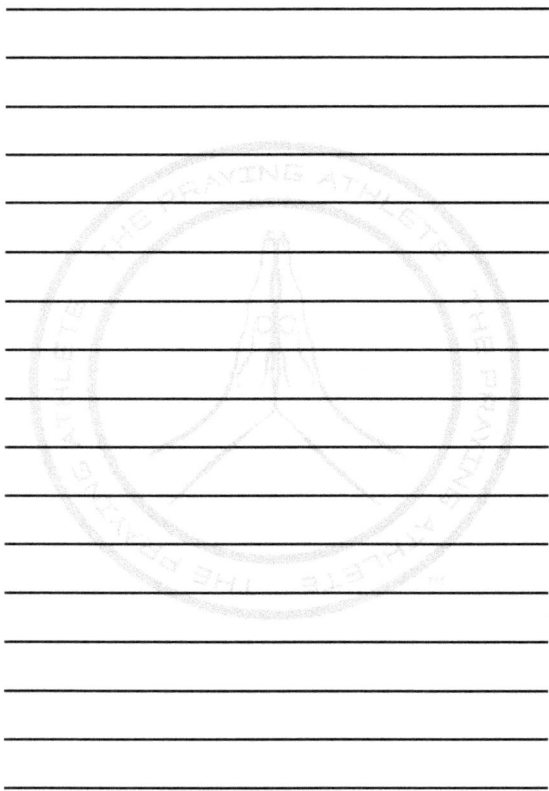

_____

_____

_____

_____

_____

_____

_____

_____

_____

_____

_____

_____

_____

_____

_____

_____

_____

_____

_____

_____

_____

_____

_____

_____

_____

_____

_____

_____

_____

_____

_____

_____

_____

_____

MY QUOTES

_____

_____

_____

_____

_____

_____

_____

_____

_____

_____

_____

_____

_____

_____

_____

_____

_____

_____

_____

_____

_____

_____

_____

_____

_____

_____

_____

_____

_____

_____

_____

_____

ACKNOWLEDGEMENTS

I want to acknowledge and say thank you to all those that
helped with this project:

Nadia Guy
Ashlyn Helms
My Mom & Dad

All of my NFL Clients, current and former, that have
encouraged me to share these words with others.

ABOUT
TPA

The Praying Athlete is a movement that creates an organic culture of prayer through an uplifting community and authentic conversation.

For more information, visit our website **www.theprayingathlete.com**.

Follow us on social media.

:camera: @ThePrayingAthlete

:bird: @Praying_Athlete

:f: @ThePrayingAthlete

COLLECT ALL

8 VOL.

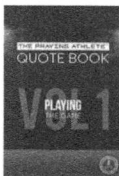

Our first volume of *The Praying Athlete Quote Book* addresses the topic of playing the game. Quotes and thoughts from Robert B. Walker, paired with Scripture from God's Word, allow readers to get a good idea about what playing a good game looks like.

Our second volume of *The Praying Athlete Quote Book* addresses the topic of teamwork. Quotes and thoughts from Robert B. Walker, paired with Scripture from God's Word, allow readers to understand what it means to be a good teammate and surround yourself with people who lift you up.

Our third volume of *The Praying Athlete Quote Book* addresses the topic of growth & preparation for the future. Quotes and thoughts from Robert B. Walker, paired with Scripture from God's Word, allow readers to know that even though the future is uncertain, there is a plan and purpose for everyone.

Our fourth volume of *The Praying Athlete Quote Book* addresses the topic of keeping the right mentality. Quotes and thoughts from Robert B. Walker allow readers to understand how staying in the right mindset can improve overall performance.

Our fifth volume of *The Praying Athlete Quote Book* addresses the topic of staying motivated. Quotes and thoughts from Robert B. Walker allow readers to become motivated to accomplish their goals, even when they feel they are not up to the task.

Our sixth volume of *The Praying Athlete Quote Book* addresses the topic of personal accountability. Quotes and thoughts from Robert B. Walker allow readers to think about how they can better themselves. Whether its ending a bad habit or saying no to anything that may hurt themselves or others, staying accountable will benefit one's character and performance.

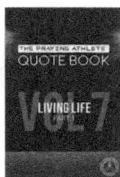

Our seventh volume of *The Praying Athlete Quote Book* addresses the topic of living life. This volume is the first part in a two part living life series. Quotes and thoughts from Robert B. Walker give readers a better understanding of how to live life to the fullest.

Our eighth volume of *The Praying Athlete Quote Book* addresses the topic of living life. This volume is the second part in a two part living life series. Quotes and thoughts from Robert B. Walker give readers a better understanding of how to live life to the fullest.

CHECK OUT OUR

THE PRAYING ATHLETE™
PHOTOGRAPHY
QUOTE BOOKS

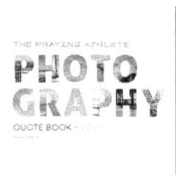

VOL. 1

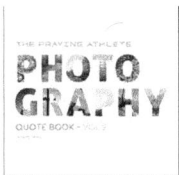

VOL. 2

VOL. 3

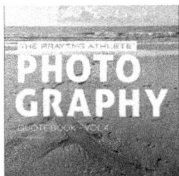

VOL. 4

*The Praying Athlete Photography Quote Book*s celebrate God's glory and magnificence through His creation. They contain photos taken by Robert B. Walker, paired with his words of wisdom, motivation, and inspiration.

FOR MORE INFO AND MERCHANDISE, PLEASE VISIT
WWW.THEPRAYINGATHLETE.COM

www.ingramcontent.com/pod-product-compliance
Lightning Source LLC
Chambersburg PA
CBHW071746020426
42331CB00008B/2199